THE BEST
NEW BRITISH
AND IRISH
POETS
2017

JUDGED, WITH AN
INTRODUCTION, BY
LUKE KENNARD
SERIES EDITOR
TODD SWIFT

THE BEST
NEW BRITISH
AND IRISH
POETS
2017

 **EYEWEAR** PUBLISHING

First published in 2017
by Eyewear Publishing Ltd
Suite 333, 19-21 Crawford Street
Marylebone, London W1H 1PJ
United Kingdom

Cover design and typeset by Edwin Smet
Printed in England by TJ International Ltd, Padstow, Cornwall

ISBN 978-1-911335-48-1

Eyewear wishes to thank Jonathan Wonham
for his generous patronage of our press.

WWW.EYEWEARPUBLISHING.COM

Dedicated to
the memory of the
poets Brigit Pegeen Kelly,
CD Wright, DG Jones, Geoffrey Hill,
Jim Harrison, Leonard Cohen,
Yves Bonnefoy, Derek Walcott,
Okla Elliott, Thomas Lux and Tom
Raworth who have all died
in the past few months.

TABLE OF CONTENTS

INTRODUCTION

Whenever I talk to my students about poetry anthologies I tell them that much of the attendant controversy concerns reputation and status anxiety. Did poets included in *The New Poetry* go on to great things because the editors made the right call and predicted their potential? Or did their inclusion in that anthology facilitate the great things by legitimising their names above many others? Either way there are a lot of hurt feelings and a ticker-tape parade of comments streams in which to vent them. This book, I like to think, is different. These are fifty poets yet to publish their first full collections (although I suspect this will not be the case for very long) and I had no names or publishing histories or anything contextual. It was solely the work. It always is, really, and anyone who writes seriously knows this. The rest is a distraction.

Competitions and anthologies of this kind are primarily self-selecting; the writers have to hear about the project and voluntarily submit their work and, as the editor, you wait and hope for a broad, varied and representational crop. I'm happy to report that I read approximately one thousand poems in the anonymised selection process. Deciding which of the fifty would make the final anthology was, at times, a painful process. Actually, I've always hated it when writers exaggerate things like that. Was it pain on the level of your currency being so devalued that you have to queue for three hours to buy a small bag of flour for all of the Venezuelan bolívars in your wallet? No. Was it even pain on the level of dashing your toes against the base of an old dresser mirror because your study is also the room where you keep most of your landlord's furniture? No, although that did happen halfway through the adjudication and helped to put things in perspective. For the most part I was sitting in a comfortable office chair, reading poems. There were many which demanded re-reading, a surplus that I felt I couldn't do without, and a very real deficit of anything which might have been easily rejectable. Without exception these were poets who had worked and worked on their technique, who had published poems in established journals, and who were fully aware of their potential readers and the experience, provocation and inspiration they might give them.

The final selection represents a foretaste of some of the most exciting new and emerging talents on the poetic scene in the UK and Ireland. I'd like to claim that the variation in tone, technique and form was by design, but in the end it didn't need to be: it was already there within the one thousand, waiting to be collated. A further happy accident is quite how well sequenced the fifty poems presented in these pages seem to be, which is remarkable considering they are arranged in order of author surname. I was delighted to find that we close so fittingly on Kate Wise's devastating, intertextual 'Death Comes Asking', a poem which spirals out to its declarative, terminal conclusion. And what better introduction than Paul Asta's 'Apiarist's Chest', which builds in haunting, elegant couplets, mixing memory, desire and family history with a generosity of spirit that welcomes the reader to the rest of the book.

Each of the forty-eight poems in between gave me something new, something urgent; they were easy for me to say yes to, to struggle with, re-read and re-read, and say yes to again: from the fragmented remix of Charlie Baylis' excerpts from 'Fifty Shades of Prufrock', which teases you but does not grant you the right to smile, to the painterly precision of Daniel Bennett's 'Monsoon (Landscape)', a powerfully evoked place and unusual atmospheric condition created with hallucinatory clarity. If there's something which unites all of the poets presented here it's their attention to detail, the resonant images which stay with you and bring character and situation to life. This is as present in the tangents of the captivating monologue in Niall

Bourke's 'Marbletown' as it is in the heart-breaking, raw yet controlled entreaty of Jo Burns' 'Places Your Children Should Never See' and Alan Buckley's spiritual exegesis of a brief moment of near-intimacy in 'Miracle'. I responded immediately to the filmic dramatisation of self-consciousness and performance in Jenna Clake's witty, concise 'Girls in Cars', and found a similar sense of meticulous social observation in Simon Collings' pitch-perfect prose poem 'The Apartment'; two very different voices which nonetheless complement each other like a double A-side.

I'm always drawn to prose poems, the form being my particular academic niche, and the examples herein are enviably assured. 'A Chaotic Spray-Effect Print of Tipp-ex on a School Bag' by Harriet Creelman captures the form's imaginative leaps and is vivid memoir, like a combination of Heaney's *Stations* and Stein's *Tender Buttons*. Susannah Dickey's 'Jellyfish Parents' filters memory through a particular, painfully funny and poignant theme – astute, bracingly honest and gorgeous. John McGhee's 'Superkafka and its Impact on Industrial Relations', perhaps the only dystopian/utopian piece here, takes the fabulist tradition to new territory with the urgency of its satire and keen wit.

Elaine Cosgrove's 'Firemen Waiting' deftly portrays a period of incongruous stillness and calm with concise lyricism and tension; a mood which continues in the linguistic intensity of Anne Cousins' 'Hare'; both poems capture a specific place and time in an original way which immediately caught my attention. The hare is one of many beasts to leap out of these pages, and the natural world with its flora and fauna is evoked with equal felicity to very different ends. The birds in Emma Danes' 'Different Woods' are the catalyst for a glowing, dangerous recollection, at once strange and familiar. Majella Kelly's 'Anadromous Vocabulary' replaces Hughes's 'Pike' for me as the most breathtaking piscine poem ever written, and Daniella

Moritz reclaims the figure of the crow as her own in 'I Am The Handmaid', visionary, insistent and hymnal. The bull in Andrew Giles' brutally insightful ekphrastic poem is as subtextual as it is in the Francis Bacon poem which inspired it, whereas the peacock in Rachel Piercey's stunning 'An Overblown Poem About Love' functions as metaphor, metonym and, well, a particularly irritating peacock in its own right.

Whether they focus on the local or the global, the poems reach the parts of our minds we too often leave dormant. Jody Porter's 'Look' is a bright, exhilarating love letter to London and its *flaneurs*, with the finest description of the Thames I've had the pleasure to read. Just as Jessica Mookherjee's 'Vernal Equinox' finds a profound and affecting connection in a conversation with the narrator's car mechanic, Matthew Paul's 'Duckwalking in West Berlin' takes us through the city and its political history, all the more pertinent for its casual, personable delivery. You'll feel like you've been present with the poet in both locations. Emma Must's 'Notes on the Use of the Austrian Scythe' is a bravura extended and evocative historical account that echoes (or swishes) all the way to the current reader; just as Samuel Prince's 'The Man From Cooma' is so richly brought to life behind his rattan fly curtain. 'Lone Man Stories' by Sarah Sibley portrays a different rural landscape and another kind of eccentric loner, shot through with the eerie appeal of childhood memory.

Of course we are ever present in the landscape, behind the camera or in plain sight with our fears, interpretations and ambivalence. Charlotte Eichler's 'At Mirror Lake' sends the moon through paroxysms of brilliant metaphor in finding its relational kernel: 'We thought we knew / how things like day and night / and love would work.' Not all places are physical. Edward

Doegar's 'Voyeurism' ranges far across the globe in its thoughtful contemplation of the communion and frustration of camaraderie in the online age, while Robin Houghton's 'She Discovered the Internet' evokes our era of increasing detachment with both humour and urgency.

This undertow of love and hate and irritation can be brought up in the mix when exploring the compelling strangeness of modern life. Joe Lines' 'It Talks' is a splendidly uncanny take on the educational setting, discomfiting in both its plausibility and surrealism, its reappropriation of official language and the heart beating beneath. Anna Kisby's 'Late Home After Latin' begins with a Classical education which enriches the narrator's life with its wild transgressions, impervious to gossip and alive to the world. Samantha Roden turns the poet's gaze and the tables on the therapeutic relationship in 'Shove Your Tissues' with a fiercely defiant incisiveness. 'Unreserved Coach B' finds meaning and reverberations of character in seemingly casual interactions on a train journey, and Matthew Rice's 'At the Lights' arrests our motion and attention in such a brief, significant moment I can't believe whole collections haven't been dedicated to it. A good poem should always leave you wishing you'd come up with the idea first.

I fell in love as deeply with the sinister gothic overtones of Elizabeth O'Connell-Thompson's 'Invitation Only' as I did with the unassuming affection of James Peake's 'The Middle Places'. I am jealous of any poet who can write a line like 'I love it when you relax with your legs across me' , but both of these concise poems felt loaded with a subtext that haunts you after the final line. I found a similar thing in Deborah Turnbull's 'Foundling', which worries the boundary between nurture and manipulation with a persuasive narrative voice.

The range of formal practice was also inspiring. The structured free verse of Maeve Henry's 'Blood Lines' vividly draws on centuries of medical innovation, its vocabulary and struggle, in three sections. Paul Nash's 'Migrant in Dagenham Park Alley' uses accomplished terza rima in a pointedly detailed character study. Richard O'Brien's 'Hammam' similarly revitalises iambic pentameter and, as it does so, lets us in to a private reflection on cleansing, otherness and travel. The epistolary candour of Simon Middleton's 'Love Note to a Donor Father' was blazing in its honesty and sincerity.

Every poem made an emotional and intellectual impact on me, whether it was quiet and meditative or shockingly direct in its exploration of trauma and loss. The radical empathy of Adele Fraser's 'Autistic Girl in Home Economics Class', for instance, left me reeling, as did the devastating confessional reflection of Geraldine O'Kane's 'Stark…', and Lauren Pope's 'Miscarriage', which hits just as hard in its harrowingly apt allegories. Three poems I will be re-reading for years to come.

I was also pleased to see poets who work on the frontier between lyric poetry and innovation, such as Thomas Crompton's 'Orion //' the deceptive Black Mountain minimalism of which opens the mind to the stars while keeping our feet firmly on the ground. Antony Huen's 'The Houses' takes in art history, relationships and decoration in its exquisitely sparse lines, incisive on the human relationship to the great art of the past. Similarly, what stands out in Carolyn Waudby's 'Dali's Rose' is her ability to dig beneath the surface of Surrealism and find the beauty and humanity which still survives, like a well-chosen detail on a broader canvas. Jack Nicholls' 'The Dolphin Sings a Love Song' collages language from the works of Dan Brown to create a seamless, surreal and enchanting (and brilliantly funny) new voice. James

Trevelyan's 'Cougar' finds inspiration in a similarly unlikely source, crafting a serious, somehow heart-rending poem out of the call signs in *Top Gun*. The direct address to the reader in Ken Evans' 'Playing Dead' is a hypnotic exercise in imagination and compassion, and the second person instruction manual of Luke Smith's 'Artmaking for Young Men' pushes the boundaries of advice and self-awareness with a subtle intelligence.

Integrity, for a writer, means to create something which you yourself would be thrilled to discover and read if you happened across it in a bookshop, in a journal, in an anthology; that's your duty to yourself and to the many like-minded readers you'll find by honouring it. Maybe it's rare to really hit that (it certainly is for me, hence my terrible laxity at sending out submissions of individual poems), but all fifty of the poets here are getting it exactly right in fifty different ways. I hope that you'll find as much to delight you here as I did.

LUKE KENNARD, 2017

PAUL ASTA

was born in South Korea.
He is a bookbinder and writer from the
Chicago suburbs who serves as a Poetry Editor
for *Hobart*. He is currently studying Creative
Writing at University College Cork on a
Fulbright Scholarship. He has received awards
from the National Society of Arts and Letters
and the Academy of American Poets, as well as
fellowships from the Vermont Studio Center
and Indiana University, Bloomington where
he earned his MFA in Poetry. His work can be
found or is forthcoming in *Ninth Letter,*
The Journal, Dostoyevsky Wannabe,
and others.

APIARIST'S CHEST

— Mark Rothko, White Center (Yellow, Pink and Lavender on Rose), 1950

I.
I do not know the colour
of hunger, or where it is kept

murmuring like persistent bees
surveying the garden, but I know

this is not a history of geography.
In the backyard, my father stands

at the center of winter, the look
of sleep in his eyes: says, *son*

*if you're listening, this
is my body broken for you.*

II.
I will find my father's torso
in the back of the closet,

wrapped in burlap and stained
with dirt; holding on to the earth

where we buried my grandfather
underneath the willow trees.

I will find his arms in the bed
of the piano, resting themselves

on familiar keys. His head tucked
away in the field, whispering

into the wind. *This is the voice
I've heard calling in the night.*

And somewhere beyond the hum
of electricity and the consequence

of rain, I will find his legs discarded
among the train tracks, working

their way back home.

III.
There is still room left
to explore: what remains

of the body are craters
dispersed over the landscape,

scars which remind us of the songs
we used to sing. After they took

one of my grandfather's lungs,
I remember him saying,

*I finally feel like there's room
to breathe.* How the torso

is more like a hive, an open
cavity. A void waiting

to be filled. How I have
only been stung by a bee

once, right in the chest.

CHARLIE BAYLIS

was born in Nottingham.
His critical writing has been published
in *Stride, Neon* and *Sabotage Reviews*. His poetry
has been nominated for two Pushcart Prizes, the
Forward Prize, and the Queen's Ferry Press's
Best Small Fictions. He was (very briefly) a flash
fiction editor for *Litro*. He has published two
pamphlets: *Elizabeth* (Agave Press) and
*Hilda Doolittle's Carl Jung
T-shirt* (Erbacce).

FROM FIFTY SHADES OF PRUFROCK

i
Anastasia. Christian. Seattle
tinkles her porcelain teeth. Prufrock
exits a black Mercedes-Benz.

'Miss Cavanagh, I have a strange feeling

I mean Miss Steele'. Prufrock, J Alfred Prufrock
scatters his laughter among the rich, scatters his rice
among the poor.
'Mr Prufrock, to what do you attribute your success?'

'I have learnt to listen to the mermaids' song.'

ii
Anastasia: *'Come here Prufrock, go away Prufrock'*
He comes and goes, crawling on his toes
arranging peaceful afternoons at the Heathman Hotel.

iii
Mr Prufrock takes his coffee with cream
he will not answer to what this means.

iv
November, narwhals; Prufrock among the penguins
'Miss Steele will you sign this little letter, later
you may leave me in my arms.'

Tinned peaches on an autumnal lawn.

Prufrock plays the piano silhouetted by the cityscape.
He never does any work. Mia (his sister) comes home from Paris.
Prufrock remembers the happy times.

v
Anastasia's safe words are 'red' and 'yellow'.

vi
Anastasia. Christian. The end.
When the plot is this bad, no
you do not have the right to smile.

DANIEL BENNETT

was born in Shropshire
and lives and works in London.
His poems have appeared in a number
of places, most recently in *Structo,*
The Stinging Fly, and *The Literateur.*
He's also the author of the
novel *All the Dogs.*

MONSOON (LANDSCAPE)

Lazy water monitors roll along the bank,
under green sunlight. A man in red
tends to the paddy field beneath the mountain

his steps seemingly random among the stalks
his industry patient, hypnotic.
We are new here, ill-defined.

Later, rain appears over the coconut trees,
these broad fins, like splayed herringbones,
the grey sky turning as dull as their bark.

A family of monkeys descends,
cracking through branches and thicket,
to cross the borders of the paddy field

with wary meticulousness. These tropical days
of guilty indolence. We snack on Chinese oranges
the pippy flesh fizzing like sherbet

but the landscape requires our disappearance
so we lose ourselves to lazy heat,
like abstracted lizards rolling in cool water.

My postcards will read, 'I have dissolved.'
In the distance, the storm is muted,
and sounds like water, trapped in the inner ear.

NIALL BOURKE

is from Kilkenny, Ireland,
but now lives in London. He teaches
English Literature at St. Michael's College in
Bermondsey, and in 2015 he finished an MA in
Creative Writing and Teaching at Goldsmiths
University of London. His poetry and prose
have been published in a number of journals and
magazines in the UK and Ireland, including *The
Galway Review, South Bank Poetry, Magma,*
and *Ink Sweat & Tears.* In 2015 he was longlisted
for The Short Story Competition and has
been twice shortlisted for the Over The
Edge New Writer Of The Year. He has also
been shortlisted for the 2015 Costa
Short Story Award.

MARBLETOWN

Stanislas Murphy, drunk to grubbuggery,
crawls into a cab and begins bending the ear
offa the in-work driver (an out-of-work bricklayer)
about a TV show where a politician claimed
five thousand euro for office toilet roll.
The driver's getting angry
because the Lonnergans (two n's, mind)
are lying on a square of carpet in the middle of the road
and baytin the bells off each other using lengths of timber.
Again. After they get dragged home by the mammy
(total quarehawk) the driver tells Stanislas
sure the banks only have the country ruined, ruined,
and, anyways, didn't her cousin hear that the politician
had been forced to sniff The Bishop's sandwiches
when he was a child (when the politician was a child that is,
not The Bishop. The Bishop was a child once, of course,
he played the harpsichord with precocious talent
and lived in the house with bougainvillea in the garden.
But that's another story). Rome caught wind
of The Bishop's olfactory predilections
and packed him off to a parish in Guatemala
to oversee the making of charitable packed lunches.
Stanislas laughs at this so hard that his all-day breakfast roll
splutters out over the dash and so the driver turfs him out;
half for acting the maggot/half because she vowed
to never allow another French bejaysus loaf in her car again
after that bleedin goal in Paris.
Stanislas swears he's done with drink and then falls asleep in a ditch.
In the morning either 1) the guy driving the ditch trimmer
doesn't see him there and chops him up. The grief is palpable.
Or 2) Stanislas wakes up *before* the trimmer
but still too late for work

so gets a fierce bollockin off the husband.
After a right auld barney they collapse
weeping into each other's arms because, deep down,
they both know that sure the banks only have the country ruined,
ruined and, sure, anyways, how is anyone meant to make a living
anymore at all.

ALAN BUCKLEY

was brought up on Merseyside.
His debut pamphlet, *Shiver*, was a Poetry Book
Society choice in 2009, and his second pamphlet,
The Long Haul, has recently been published by
HappenStance. For the last five years, he has
been a school writer-in-residence for First Story.
He also works as a psychotherapist for a refugee
charity in Oxford.

MIRACLE

I'm both – the one who resurrects
and also the corpse, wrapped
in white linen. I stare
at the bedroom curtains

as dawn leaks in at their edges.
My mind's a tomb, shut
with a boulder, beyond
which the other me weeps.

Sometimes we pull it off,
give the punters a show.
I strut my stuff on the big stage.
But mostly there's no miracle,

just compromise, days spent
in a café off the main drag,
our coffees cooling before us.
We've so much, so little to say.

Our hands are beached fish
that twitch on the table.
If someone could only move
that ketchup bottle, who knows,

they might even touch.

JO BURNS

was born in Maghera, County
Derry, Northern Ireland, and has resided in
Chile, Scotland, England, and now Germany.
She dabbles in German poetry translation while
raising three children. Her poems have been
published by numerous journals worldwide,
most recently *A New Ulster*, *Poetry Breakfast*,
The Galway Review, *The Honest Ulsterman*,
The Irish Literary Times, *Poetry NI P.O.E.T*
Anthology, *The Literateur*, and *Lakeview*
International Journal of Arts
and Literature.

PLACES YOUR CHILDREN SHOULD NEVER SEE

That place where mothers never switched
the radio on again. Where they froze
rushed moments before they closed *that* door

to school bags and swinging plaited pigtails.
Where cold snapped busy *Dunblane* kitchens,
as news hurled white space into black.

Where life was air-sucked to resettle in soot.
Where updates crackled to lay numb
on frozen, turned-off, stations.

Or where children, ash-smothered, headlined.
A place where veins filled fat with hoarfrost
and throbbed to beats of still falling snow

and absence as *Chernobyl* cracked.
Where florid sobs of icy geigers flowed
in sheets of caesium, strontium, iodine.

Where beta burns and marbled thyrocytes
cooked in blinks of burst and scatter.
Or a *Buchenwald* (even Goethe's oak stood silent).

A place that strangles your pink young lung.
Chambers of a red hot heart. A *Raqqa,* or Bastille day *Nice.*
Places where you will always be inexorably wrong.

You are primed arrows in my leathered hand,
and I know each future aim will send you near it all.
My own heart the target. The bow reverbs.

Children, close your eyes to the cold gravity of our moon.
I'll switch the clock back to when you had it mild.
Climb back. Curl softly into my womb.

JENNA CLAKE

is studying for a PhD in Creative Writing. Her research focuses on the feminine and Feminist Absurd in twenty-first century British and American poetry. She is also the Poetry and Arts Editor for the *Birmingham Journal of Literature and Language*. Her poetry has appeared in *Poems in Which*, *The Bohemyth*, *Queen Mob's Teahouse,* and more. Her debut collection, *Fortune Cookie,* won the Melita Hume Poetry Prize and will be published by Eyewear in 2017.

GIRLS IN CARS

The thing is, we're driving around and N keeps on hitting
me in the face with her elbow as she tries to hang on
to the scarf wrapped round her head. L wants the windows
down: *I want us to look like we're in the movies,* she shouts
over the wind and the radio. In the movies, your hair
doesn't stick to your lip gloss. N's wearing sunglasses too,
even though it's dark, and she tells us that she's channelling
her inner Hepburn but I know that she's dyed the ends
of her hair blonde and it's gone wrong. When she told
me, she said *ombre* like it was the name of her boyfriend.
D has stayed silent the whole time. She keeps on checking
the rear-view mirror like she expects to see her father staring
right back at her. We aren't wearing our seatbelts – we never do
– so when D brakes hard my knees go into the back of L's
chair. We're at the traffic lights now. N wants to drive around
for longer but the rest of us are ready. You can tell when L's
ready: she sings louder than the rest of us. Some men pull up
next to the car. They wind down their windows, lean out.
We look ahead as they take pictures of us on their phones.

SIMON COLLINGS

has worked in international
development for most of his professional life.
He has published short stories, poems and music
reviews in a variety of print and electronic
media. His poems have appeared in *Stride,
Ink Sweat & Tears, Brittle Star, New Walk, The
Interpreter's House* and other journals.
He lives in Oxford.

THE APARTMENT

On entering the apartment I was surprised to find that a number of the guests had arrived before me. They had evidently been there for some time, and were making themselves at home, lounging in armchairs or sitting on cushions on the floor. I had expected to be early, deliberately arriving in advance of the appointed time in order to enjoy a few private moments with our host, and to be in possession of the territory as it were when the others arrived. On my way there I had pictured the apartment, which I had not previously visited, visualising its pale blue striped wallpaper, the collection of antique carriage clocks, the paintings. I had seen photographs, and knew of his tastes from our frequent conversations, and the rooms were in many respects exactly as they had been described, though in other ways disconcertingly unfamiliar. G came over to greet me, and his manner was as open and genial as it had always been. I had thought of him as reclusive, a man who did not easily admit others into his company. But the presence of the other guests now left me unsure of my position and I found myself looking down at the carpet and noticing to my dismay that the lace of my right shoe had come untied.

ELAINE COSGROVE

is from County Sligo, Ireland.
Her work has been published by
The Stinging Fly, The Penny Dreadful, The Bohemyth, and *New Binary Press*. Elaine was a 2015 Poetry Ireland Introductions poet. Her work was highly commended in The Gregory O'Donoghue Prize, and long-listed for the 2016 *London Magazine* Poetry Prize. Elaine works in the community and voluntary sector.
Her first collection will be published
in 2017 by Dedalus Press.

FIREMEN WAITING

Shutters are up, front of station – engines gleam, exposed.
Two firemen puck a sliothar to pass time
in the half-time between emergencies.
The ball rises, thick stitched moon over traffic light, red.
The pure boldness of these responsible men, spilling out over
the curbs – their sniggers at a tugged warning from an older one
who waters sweetpea plants on the station's windowsills:
'Careful on that road, lads,' as he tilts the typical green can.
Autumn's air wraps her hands around us – dice of delicacy
under wire, coil, tank, hose. Chill will come, and we'll always
know this. Hear their attention in the green dip, the go of sirens –

ANNE COUSINS

has had poems published in *The Stinging Fly, The SHOp, The Honest Ulsterman, The Irish Literary Review,* and *Skylight 47*. She completed her MA in Creative Writing (UCD) in 2013. Her first collection, *Redress* (a work in progress), was shortlisted in the Patrick Kavanagh Poetry Competition in 2015 and again in 2016. In 2016, she featured in Poetry Ireland's Introductions Series. She also writes memoir and local history essays for 'Sunday Miscellany' on RTE Radio 1.

HARE

After the nuns left
we noticed that a hare –
a beast of a fellow
with strong back legs,
proud ears
and a thick fur coat
– had moved in.

Superior now,
our hare lays waste
to what is left
of the lay-sister's
herb garden, savages
Reverend Mother's salad bed
and emerges fragrant
from the Mistress of Novices'
lavender border.

Sweet and sated,
it bounds through the cloisters –
not a chance of prayer
passing its cloven lip –
its soul long saved.

HARRIET CREELMAN

is a poet and producer, and is
one of the six London Laureates for
2015-2016. She has read her work widely,
from Queen Elizabeth Hall to Ronnie Scott's,
BOXPARK to StAnza. She was a founding
member of Burn After Reading and is co-
director of TOAST– a Spread the Word/
Arts Council-backed poetry organization that
supports poets beyond the emerging
stage of their careers.

A CHAOTIC SPRAY-EFFECT PRINT OF TIPP-EX ON A SCHOOL BAG
(Rory Parnell Mooney A/W '16)

Ease continues to be favoured in this season's clothing's build, whilst it continues to be something that feels too treacherous in life, like motorbikes or honesty. The path of least resistance is how burglars entered the flat and stole my signet ring, which I probably deserved. It is how these boys move. Frictionless. There was a chaotic spray-effect print of Tipp-Ex on my GCSE Geography exam and I think that Tipp-Ex is a perfect metaphor for life. Clown class taught me that crying and laughing looks the same on stage or from a distance. It is how these boys cry. Ambiguously. From the back seat of the classroom, these belts look like anchor ropes or maybe the lost string of a balloon. Buckles are not de rigueur this year and I learned in long white socks that absence is how we measure. I weigh a head by how much water it displaces. I weigh a heart by how much of me it displaces. And I want to sew up this nothingness. It is how these boys are. Weightless. Measureless. Scrawled across their patchwork are happy biro words of *tomorrow, tomorrow and tomorrow and I want to throw the script at them and re-rehearse, shouting nothing or today, or bow my head like school and whisper amen amen amen*

THOMAS CROMPTON

lives and works in Lancashire
where he grew up. Publishing here and there
over the last few years, he most recently put out
a collaborative digital piece called *png* through
The New Fire Tree Press; he is also currently
working on a run of hand-made pamphlets,
set for release in the near future.

ORION //

dear Orion,

some angels   speak in
touches

           the motorway
           the kennels
           the choke

           of pollen
           banging on my window

since you went away
I have
this light   to bathe in
& like a crow
I have kept the shock

for the last few words
we are dying

pink star

luv tom

EMMA DANES'

pamphlet *Dress of Shadows* was a
winner in the Poetry Business Book & Pamphlet
Competition 2012/13. Her poems have won the
Hamish Canham Prize and the Poetry Society
Stanza Poetry Competition, and been published
in anthologies and magazines including *CAST:
The Poetry Business Book of New Contemporary
Poets* (Smith|Doorstop) and *The Best
British Poetry 2011* (Salt). Emma currently
works freelance in publishing.
She lives with her family in Ely.

DIFFERENT WOODS

The birds have whetted their voices.
They snip minute shapes from the air,
unfold a pierced-work symmetry.

There's a brittleness at the edge
of experience. As a child
I put a finger in the blue

flame of our cooker and, gently,
to the mirror's hairline crack.
That is how I learned not to touch

beautiful things, why I'm out here
in these different woods, checking
for the burn, the fault line in the song.

– first appeared in *Magma*

SUSANNAH DICKEY

was born in 1992 in Belfast,
Northern Ireland. She is currently
in her final year of studying for a BA in English
with Creative Writing at Queen's University
Belfast. Her work has been published in
the *London Journal of Fiction, Funhouse
Magazine* and *The Open Ear.*

JELLYFISH PARENTS

I

We go to the beach when I am a child. When I wade into water, the colour of a dead tooth, staccato waves the shape of parentheses slap me as I jump. I wear a full-length black body sock and neoprene shoes that fill with water on entry and slosh. The sand is an open grave of jellyfish corpses. I poke a holographic afterbirth with a newborn twig and watch it undulate. The bare bone exposed between wetsuit and shoe is the bit that later protests with the pain of jellyfish stings under the hot water of the shower. It's a small price to pay for feeling worldly.

II

The night before I leave for university we have dinner in a Thai restaurant. All they have in common is me, and I want to leave but also don't want to leave so they watch me watch the jellyfish in the tank. I say 'Jellyfish don't have brains', and she says 'Just like your father, eh?' because he had lost the car earlier among a sea of cars in the multi-storey car park. He is sitting next to me and I feel him stiffen but he says nothing so I pretend to stifle a giggle in an attempt to placate but even this feels like a small act of betrayal. She says 'Expand on that then', and I realise I can't remember anything else I read except that jellyfish reproduce by external fertilisation but I don't like to bring up sex because she will say something snide or he will say something mildly inappropriate in an attempt to appropriate the language of young people. I just say 'That's it', and she tells me I will never be a lawyer if I can't expand on a topic or an argument, and I suspect she knows like I know that I will never be a lawyer.

III

'The jellyfish parent is a permissive parent'. I read this on a website devoted to parenting styles while I idly run a finger around the swollen dune of my abdomen. I think of the polyp forming inside me. I am six months into a nine month gestation period and it occurs to me that most jellyfish do not live longer than six months, do not wonder what becomes of their offspring, do not wonder anything.

IV

When I am 4 she is rendered incapable of further reproduction. The day we wait outside her hospital room I ask 'Will she get to keep the womb?' He is holding chocolates and I am holding a balloon with trailing fronds that look like tentacles. It's not for her, but for me, for being brave and well-behaved.

'No', he says, 'It's too ugly.'

– first appeared in *Ambit*

EDWARD DOEGAR's
poems, reviews and translations
have appeared in various magazines,
including *Poetry Review, Poetry London,
Prac Crit* and *Poetry Wales*. He's a fellow of
the Complete Works programme, a scheme
promoting diversity in British poetry, and
six of his poems are featured in the Bloodaxe
anthology *Ten: The New Wave*. He works at
The Poetry Society and is currently
on the assistant editor programme
at *The Rialto*.

VOYEURISM

My friend has become
My anecdotal acquaintance
Our man in Afghanistan
I exaggerate for effect
In Pakistan he's a pixelated blip
On the unagreed map
A fragmentary man who I make
Plans with on Skype
Plans I won't keep to meet him
In the theatre of when
That is his life
War frightens us differently
Now he's somewhere else
Eastern Ukraine
Always where he needn't be
I tell someone I barely know
How I lose track of him
How I lost track of him once
In the Louvre at seventeen
How in that hour
All I saw were lookalikes
Admiring Roman copies
Of Greek attitudes
While he looked at the statues

– first appeared in *Ambit*

CHARLOTTE EICHLER's

work has appeared in magazines
such as *The Rialto, Agenda, And Other
Poems,* and *The Interpreter's House.* She has
been shortlisted for the Bridport and Flambard
Poetry Prizes and was commended in the 2016
Battered Moons poetry competition. She
lives in West Yorkshire and works as
an editor and medievalist.

AT MIRROR LAKE

it took us by surprise, how fast the moon rose –
a stone thrown from the cliff

floating loose in hot blue sky.
We asked why, as if its grey bloom

in the day was extraordinary.
Our words were clipped, unkind with fatigue.

I watched your profile, the suddenly unfamiliar
curve of your nose. We thought we knew

how things like day and night
and love would work.

I held you too hard and my nails
made chilly little moons along your arm.

– first appeared in *The Rialto*

KEN EVANS

gained a Distinction in his
poetry Master's from Manchester University
in 2015. His work was longlisted in the Poetry
Society's National Competition, highly-
commended in the Bridport, and shortlisted
in the Troubadour Competition, all in 2015.
Ken's debut pamphlet was released by Eyewear
Publishing in 2016. His poems also appear in
*Envoi, Obsessed with Pipework, The Glasgow
Review of Books, The Morning Star, Island
Review,* and *Ink Sweat & Tears.*

PLAYING DEAD

Pretend you are a child
and dead. Lie on your back in the meadow,
let grass prick your flesh, the earth's damp cellar
chill your spine. Let flowers flashmob
a trouser hem. Feel your warmth drain
in the soft earth, seep across the field,
bleeding into falling light. Forget the shapes
in clouds children find, see instead sky
through dead men's eyes, a red absence.
Ignore the charm-world of mortgage, lawn, car,
imagine instead death tickling the inside
of your unbuttoned blouse. A stag beetle clambers
the damp hairs on your wrist, drinks the sweat
from under a fingernail. Your outstretched palm
twitches on a resting pulse. An early fox
in late afternoon tracks your tumulus-curve,
the owl blinks at your flat shadow, swivels to softer
targets. Small things you only dimly hear,
scratch, scrape, shuffle across grass.
You wonder how long before things grow
over, bind you to the soil.

– first appeared in *Lighthouse*

ADELE FRASER

lives and writes in North Wales.
Her poems have appeared in *Envoi, Obsessed
with Pipework, The Interpreter's House, Ink Sweat
& Tears, Amaryllis,* and *Mslexia,* among others.
She has also had poems published in the Eyewear
anthologies *#RefugeesWelcome: Poems in a
Time of Crisis* and *#NousSommesParis.*

AUTISTIC GIRL IN HOME ECONOMICS CLASS

The wicked whisks are mixing up everything,
swirling the room and the people in it.
There are too many of them. A blender of faces,
angles, movements. My eyes are confused
and don't know which limb on which person to follow.
I am being churned. I am dizzy. Disorientated. The floor
lurches and tilts. Colours blur. Shapes lose definition
and I lose awareness of direction. Left is right and up is down.
The room is a soup and my attention has drowned.
Everyone is too loud. And I am too visible. Exposed.

In front of me, bags and bowls of foods I don't understand.
Unfamiliar scents and textures assault my senses,
wrestle them to the ground and ground them like peppers,
like planes, like nonconforming children like
myself. I am feeling anxious. I am feeling panicked.
I am feeling   sick.

The recipe I can only read, not act on. I cannot follow
instructions. I cannot equate language with objects.
I cannot process sequentially, compartmentalise chaos,
and hold linear steps in my circular head. Nor can I pretend
to enjoy this. I am the miller's daughter from *Rumpelstiltskin*,
locked in / and ordered by a powerful figure / to spin
straw into gold.

I eye the tables, battle the urge to crawl under them,
disguising my distress with exaggeration, letting everyone
think my bewilderment is comical, eliciting aid in exchange
for entertainment. It is the only card I hold.

My friend laughs. I feel relief I can control / this much,
but still I don't know *why* she laughs, why anyone would laugh
when we are being tortured essentially
and no one has noticed.

She takes the dishes from me, consults the list,
begins the alchemy (as ever, in her element).
And, easily, naturally, with a casual indifference,
she does the inexplicable, performs the miracle
of putting things together
                    like she processes the world,
squeezing experience through a neural icing tube,
focused and filtered and formed / into words.

ANDREW F GILES

currently lives and works in Bristol.
He has poems, reviews and criticism in various
journals and anthologies, most recently *The
Scotsman*, *Butcher's Dog*, and the *Journal of Iberian
and Latin American Studies*. He co-convened the
Bristol to Bath Festival of Nature Poetry Trail
2016, performing his commission for the BBC.
He researches poetry & antipsychiatry in
Spain at the University of Bristol and
is on the board of the Bristol
Poetry Institute.

FRANCIS BACON, 'STUDY OF A BULL' (1991)

We meet or fuck people all the time.
They are shaped
like desks or swivel chairs with eyes.
We are fucking so hard a dictionary
full of words speak inside us,
but where do we find out
what we would like to
know?
            This is not a solution-based approach.
There is the Protection Act,
the diseases that we catch
behind our backs.

But here we are, with the same rug of skin
that everyone has, with our fragment
of vision that so breezily fails
the structure of its own meaning,

and still we meet after the show –
in the language of in-between
faces that will all buckle like
portals. It doesn't mean that.
Damage, whatever it means.

– first appeared in *Butcher's Dog*

MAEVE HENRY

is an Irish poet who lives in Oxford.
She works in hospital administration and is
currently studying for a Master's in Creative
Writing at Oxford Brookes. Her work has been
published in various places, including *Mslexia,
The Interpreter's House,* and *Ink Sweat & Tears.*
She was longlisted for the National Poetry
Competition in 2014 and 2015. She is
married and has three children.

BLOOD LINES

I Brit Milah
He that is eight days old, born in your house,
must be circumcised or his soul shall be cut
off from his people. Yet, because the three sisters
at Sepphoris lost their first born to the perfecting
cut, Rabbi Gamaliel told the fourth she must
not circumcise her son. For in one family
the blood is loose, while in another the blood
is held fast. Blessed are You,
Lrd our Gd, King of the universe,
Who has sanctified us with Your commandments,
and commanded us concerning circumcision.

II Romanov
'A haemorrhage…without the slightest cause
from the navel of our small Alexis.' So begins
a short life, whose childhood knocks are national
disasters. Red pools linger in joints, strikes cripple.
Political fevers spike and the inherited disorder
moves from fitful remission to final crisis,
from Tsarskoye Selo to Tobolsk.

'In the evening we shot at the target, for something to do.
It's boring, but it's getting warmer.
The red guards have been here a week.'

Lyoshka's last diary entry before
Ipatiev House, place of special purpose,
its whitewashed windows nailed up in the July heat,
where, carried in his father's arms at midnight

down twenty-three steps to the basement,
his bleeding ended.

III New World
'Ordinary purging doses of sulphate of soda'
were applied to the small bleeders, the Shepherd boys,
to no great effect, Dr John Otto recorded

in the *Medical Repository* in 1803.
Later prescriptions included calcium lactate,
Witt's peptone, anaphylaxis, and the galvanic needle.
In the Fifties, peanut butter. McFarlane in Oxford
 swore by snake venom to trigger the clotting cascade.

In the year of the Civil Rights Act and *Love Me Do*,
Judith Pool scraped the muck from a defrosted bag,
and, unlike her lab mates, stuck by her results,
leaps in blood clotting requiring the human factor.
The good news – with minor adjustments for hep C,
HIV, CJD – kept coming. Cancer took Judith, at fifty-three.

– first appeared in *The Hippocrates Prize Competition 2015 Anthology*

ROBIN HOUGHTON

is published widely in magazines
including *Agenda, Bare Fiction, Poetry News,
Prole,* and *The Rialto,* and in numerous
anthologies. She won the 2013 Hamish Canham
Prize and the 2014 Stanza Competition and was
runner-up in the Plough Poetry Prize 2014. Her
pamphlet, *The Great Vowel Shift,* was published
by Telltale Press in 2014. Robin has also written
three commissioned books on blogging.

SHE DISCOVERED THE INTERNET

from *'Business Class'*

Between the red meeting room and the blue meeting room
I stopped believing in sock liners and moulded footbeds.

I no longer believed in my boss though I still admired his arms –
the section from wrist to elbow – while talking lenticular logos.

At that particular moment by the photocopier I stopped
thinking about the fall range and the thousands of shoes

travelling the world footloose and never coming in to land.
Even the lead designer – three slips of the tongue away

from calling me the *clueless marketing bitch* I clearly was –
on this day looked older and smaller and I forgot what time

zone I lived in, or how to spell my name. Somewhere between
the door of the blue meeting room, heavy with meaning –

form follows function – and the tubular chair, I stopped believing
in my hard-copy life, in cushioning, in adiprene™ and in everything

I'd learnt, or said, or done before that day. It had to stay secret.
I guarded it like a cat guards a bird with one wing: *mine, mine.*

– first appeared in *Obsessed with Pipework*

ANTONY HUEN

grew up in Hong Kong.
He received his early literary training,
and subsequently taught, at the Chinese
University of Hong Kong. Currently, he
is a PhD student at the University of York,
researching contemporary poetry in relation
to visual art. His poetry and articles have
appeared in *Cha: An Asian Literary
Journal* and elsewhere.

THE HOUSES

Yours
after Wyman Wong

I behaved as your wallpaper
but last night you tore me apart
and replaced me with Rothko's.

His

I am his table, your legs between mine.
I am his *Weeping Woman* opposite you.
I am his chair, your legs crossing mine.
I am his television.
I am his bathtub.
I am his mirror.
I am his shirt.
I am his bed.
I am his cat.

Mine

During yoga,   my body is my house

steam   from the boiling kettle

humidity drips from the ceiling

windows and doors   wide open

wind enters   and exits

the cactus

Monet's bridge

    two droplets from the tap

photos   vacated

    credit to her non-diegetic voice

MAJELLA KELLY

lives in Tuam, County Galway.
Her poetry has been placed in numerous
poetry prizes, including runner-up in the *Ambit*
Summer Competition 2016 judged by Sarah Howe
and second prize in the Dromineer Poetry
Competition 2016 judged by Collette Bryce.
She has been published in *Crannóg 41, The
Pickled Body, Quarryman,* and *Cyphers* among
others. She began a Masters in Creative
Writing at the University of Oxford
in September 2016.

ANADROMOUS VOCABULARY

#1
The words are wilted, clammy in my hand
as a bad handshake. I toss them in the Corrib,
watch them drop to the river bed

like mayfly eggs. A fingerling flips
to face the current, stills in its rippling grip, waiting
for what the river might bring her

and swallows it all – the insect nymphs,
the mollusks, the vowels and the consonants.
Three little syllables ease through her gills;

they silver, become anadromous,
develop a tolerance for saltiness.
Take us with you, they whisper, and she does.

#2
Salmon know when it is time
to come back to attend the regatta
of the duns' newly exposed wings.

They also know how to climb ladders.
Onlookers gather to watch them
take to the air – ejaculatory

as prayers – because a single drop of home
in a million gallons of seawater is erotic
to them as the breath of a lover.

For this particular fish, it is the limestone,
the lichen of St. Michael's Well. It is the sperm
of freshwater pearl mussels below the falls.

It is shed feathers of the local heron
and the landing dance of the cormorant,
where the persistent tongue of the river

laps at the lake. She makes for the sweet-spot
where the pink-tipped stamen of the hawthorn
fondles the water – inhales its almond pollen.

#3
May Day dawns and she is barely a glimmer
in a quiet pool near the riverbank,
wary of the fisherman.

My dropped words have softened
and polished in her gullet
the way waves mend sharp edges

of sea-glass. Soon, she will open her mouth
for the fly you have tied – listen,
for the soft splosh

of *I love you*, as she leaps in the dark.

– first appeared in *the Wild Atlantic Words competition anthology*

ANNA KISBY

is a Devon-based poet and archivist.
Her poems are widely published in magazines
including *Magma*, *Mslexia*, and *Poetry News*, and
anthologies including the British Library's *Alice*
anthology and Live Canon's *154: contemporary
poets respond to Shakespeare's sonnets*. She won the
Proms Poetry Competition 2016, the Havant
Poetry Competition 2016 and was commended
in the Faber New Poets Scheme 2015-16.

LATE HOME AFTER LATIN

It was Ovid that started it — all those goddesses
swollen with Jupiter's seed — spilled on legs, aswim,
in swanform, faces upturned to golden rain —
and how gently, accidentally, again and again
we nudged knees —

Here she comes, knickers round her ankles —
I try to quiet the latch but end up falling
into the undressing eyes
of all the drunken aunties with Mum
sobering up around the cup-stained pine table —

Aren't you the mucky one? —
not long since my cheeks were pinched for a spitwash
and now their eyes turn me to stone, my toes rooting
into shagpile, tights wrong-twisted — how I'd been grubbed
was all over me —

until they're reading tealeaves, fingering
tarnished earrings and I'm scrambling railway verges, blackberry
mouthed, unshod and penniless to London Bridge, falling down
in weeds (where fairies used to live) listening all night
to the pips of the crossing —

this is the city: no gods, just mortals waiting — caught
because whenever I close my eyes I see words declining, girls
turning into cows and trees, and with eyes open I see stars smearing
the sky like my own jammy face and the moon a tongue
reaching out to lick the night clean

JOE LINES

was born in Chichester in 1987
and now lives in Belfast. His poems
have been published in *Poetry Ireland Review,*
Causeway/Cabhsair, and the anthology
Urban Myths and Legends from
The Emma Press.

IT TALKS

By great application, however, I discovered the names
that were given to some of the most familiar objects
of discourse; I learned and applied the words *fire*, *milk*,
bread and *wood*. I learned also the names of the cottagers
themselves.
– Mary Shelley, *Frankenstein*

I have one atypical student
in my French class this term.
When he speaks the striplight
flickers and drumming rain
rises behind his voice.

When asked his mother tongue
he must have misunderstood,
saying it was French,
which he claims to have acquired
from farmers in Saxony;
some kind of language exchange.
He speaks highly of the experience
but the disadvantages of this
learning environment are evident.

Other issues for concern:
erratic pronunciation,
sometimes disruptive in class,
slow to master basic vocabulary
e.g. *man, woman, good, bad.*
One day he asked the meaning of
the terms *monster, wretch* and *creature.*
I told him they were synonyms.

JOHN McGHEE

lives and works in South London.
His work has appeared in
*Magma, Lighthouse, South Bank
Poetry,* and *Under the Radar.* He is
currently completing a PhD
on surrealism and
futures studies.

SUPERKAFKA AND ITS IMPACT ON INDUSTRIAL RELATIONS

Welcome to Iron Mountain's premiere underground data center facility, located 200 feet beneath rolling countryside in a former limestone mine [...] More than 2,700 employees work in this underground city spread across 145 acres.

Company website

At the town hall, I broke the news: the cavern was to be converted to a mushroom farm, potentially a park for BMXers and their crews. Over heckles, boos, I took them through the plans in detail: the conveyors, the spawners, each of the hypothetical whoop-de-doos. Bottom line, we were done with the workers and most of their golf carts. But the technicians saw it coming and rose. I was bunkered and soon hostaged, leveraged in a chokehold from the nightmare automaton Superkafka, the workers' designated spokesman. As negotiations dragged, Superkafka's doomsday logic determined me to be 'devoid of content'. Abandoned to the back-and-forth and way too brittle, the rangers found me particulated later, clogging up the switchgear.

– first appeared in *Lighthouse*

SIMON MIDDLETON
was shortlisted for the 2015
Elbow Room Prize, and was a runner-up in
the 2007 Bridport Junior Prize. His work has
previously featured in, or is forthcoming in, *The
Cadaverine*, *Ink Sweat & Tears*, *Elbow Room*, *The
Jawline Review* and *Firewords Quarterly*. Presently,
he works as a teacher of English in Dorset,
where he lives with his partner and son.

LOVE NOTE TO A DONOR FATHER

Dear #78609, I want you to know that I have chosen you
as the father.

I've thought a lot about you recently. I'm not sleeping.
I keep seeing cells quivering in dreams, full sacks
of embroidered water. They are the best half of me,

and, I think of you – the other half;
who, on paper, fit all of my criteria:
whose height and build, intelligence and medical history
are everything I have ever looked for, but never found.
We're even the same blood type.
I wonder, perhaps, whether I could love you.

But then I see all of it, and it's easier.
Not having to cling or be exposed or suffer
the indecency of intimacy, and eventually grow
further and distant, until we are old or worse.

It's strange. I want to thank you
for the child conceived in me.
That you'll never know.

But, I wonder whether – somehow, somewhere –
the ambits of lives may overlap – and wonder more
whether I will *know,* if that day ever comes
where you meet my eye on a train, or in the street
where we clumsily move in the same direction
to avoid one another's paths. That seems
a clichéd metaphor, doesn't it?

I picture the face I have fictionalised for you,
and think of Father's Day, and the name missing
from our child's first words – knowing that *this*
is the way it has to be.

JESSICA MOOKHERJEE

is originally from Wales and lives
in Kent. She is of Bengali origin. She has
poems published in a wide range of magazines,
including *Agenda, Interpreter's House,* and
Antiphon. She was shortlisted for the 2016
Fairacre New Pamphlet Competition, winner
of the 2016 Paragram Poetry Prize, and
her first pamphlet, *The Swell,* was
published in 2016 by
Telltale Press.

VERNAL EQUINOX

I got my car checked at the garage while out to get milk
for my mother, on the first day of spring.

Sunlight was in his eyes, the mechanic squinted,
offered to top up engine oil and battery fluid.

From nowhere, from under the bonnet, he mumbled
his wife was due in a few days,

and he had a stinking cold. I told him it was my birthday.
He kept chatting, told me his girlfriend miscarried

a year ago today and now she was going to have
a spring baby, a girl. He was a boy to me, a kid from Penlan,

I bet you prefer it in the Mumbles, I said – just talking...
the sun watered my eyes,

*It's good to have the sea in front of you, makes you
never want to leave,* he said, putting the Ford's bonnet down.

And your parents, I bet they're proud – well... it's all
I could bring to him, just thinking of my mother's face,

over a cup of tea, that winter in the Gower, we were
lashed with rain and I couldn't say, *Mother, I'm unhappy,*

and all she said, as she stirred sugar in her teacup, was
there will be no grandchildren.

He seemed so young in his overalls, as he wiped oil
from his hands, *my dad died when I was small, Mum*

followed a few years back. And all I could say
in that sun infested moment was...

that I wished his baby girl the very best of luck in the world,
sounding like some cut-price fairy godmother...

I didn't tell him I ached for their futures, and how I had tied us together
by this spell. We thanked each other, I drove away.

DANIELLA MORITZ

was born in Spain and educated in
France and Switzerland. Her poems
have appeared in *máquina de cantar, The Literateur,*
and other magazines. She translates Spanish
poetry and works in London.

I AM THE HANDMAID

Hello, Señor Crow, hello
gitano! Do you like the quincunx
of freckles on my bare
shoulder? Have your waterproofs
grown in yet on wingtips?
How are the card games
with Loki, Lucifer, Huehuecóyotl?
His sarsaparilla's undrinkable!
Here, let me rub my lunulae
behind your head. An old
lover would stroke and stroke
my nails til I purred like
— now don't be jealous-afraid!
Little moons make little werecrows;
ask Some Women. It beggars belief
my nursing you, your snuffle-box.

The wasted muscles, *mi tesoro*,
that crashed you into my copper
soil will not tauten, shine.

I am cursed with foresight,
cursed over with the cliché of it.

EMMA MUST,
formerly a campaigner on
environment and development issues,
is currently completing a PhD at the Seamus
Heaney Centre at Queen's University, Belfast.
She won the Templar Portfolio Award in 2014,
and her debut poetry pamphlet, *Notes on the
Use of the Austrian Scythe*, was published by
Templar in 2015. In 2016 she was
named as one of the 'Rising
Generation' by *Poetry
Ireland Review*.

NOTES ON THE USE OF THE AUSTRIAN SCYTHE

You can no more lend a man your scythe
than you can lend him your false teeth,
so take my day instead, borrow this meadow.
I'll heap sheaves of hours inside your ward
then babble about what I've learnt of mowing:
nibs and tangs and snaths, heels and toes
and edges – esoteric glossaries
for parts of tools grown rusty through disuse;
the sharpening of blades; and principles
of movement, trimming techniques, windrows, spill.
I have a hunch all this might interest you –
who drove us at weekends to run round woods,
who pointed out seabirds, steam trains, castles –
and knowing your appreciation of the technical,
if I can communicate how vital
it is to keep the hafting angle tight,
and how though the *neigung* doesn't simply
translate it can be altered with a shim
of plywood, it might transport you for an evening
from your fixed intravenous
existence where time is marked by the sickly
drip, drip, drip of antibiotics
disrupted only by the clatter of supper
sharp at six, the tea-girl's cheery 'Cuppa?
Orange squash? Hot chocolate? Champagne?'
I hesitate to dwell too long on sharpening
the blade…I'll paraphrase: with a quality
natural whetstone, never a *klumpat*,
make one complete pass from beard to point.
That's honing. Then there's peening:
to trick life from the scythe for years to come

tap the edge of the blade with a hammer,
tease it out like pastry... But time is getting tight
so what I want to finish on tonight
are those principles of movement: staying true,
the simple shift of weight from foot to foot,
keeping give in the knees and judging the lean,
meditating on how we breathe
so we avoid those unexpected blips,
the woody stumps that send our pulses skittish.
Let's focus now on minimising spill
as late sun curves around the outfield,
concentrate on holding a line,
get satisfaction from a job well done,
hope that we have learnt enough to guide us
through the mass of grass as yet uncut.

– first appeared in *Notes on the Use of the Austrian Scythe*
(Templar, 2015)

PAUL NASH

was born in London in 1946
of an English mother and an Irish father, and
moved to Limerick at the age of eight. He is
married with three adult children. He studied
English at Trinity College Dublin and received
a PhD on the poetics and politics of modernist
literature and film. He has taught in London
and also worked in the software industry. He
has been longlisted in the UK National Poetry
Competition and shortlisted in the Bridport
Competition. Also a musician, Nash records
under the name Alphasun.

MIGRANT IN DAGENHAM PARK ALLEY

The rocking horse's iron mask is still;
Gulls stand like guards beside the abandoned swings;
The candy-coloured slide glows in the chill.

The roundabout's on freeze-frame – those grey wings
Seem exiled from the barren monochrome
Of dream-world oceans to these childless things.

And now my mascot's here, a late bird's come
To settle phantom-light on the cold mane
As on seahorses in the charging foam;

Their greeting chorus, echoing human pain,
Drifts through these railings, bars of a child's world
That I'm already visiting again

As rough gusts slap my face; once a gale hurled
Over our pigeon house, and brought a stray
And ailing gull; whose life, though warmly furled

In heated towels, soon took its wild way,
Leaving a corpse-ghost, light as a starved child.
Thus homeward-tilting wings of memory weigh

Deaths great and small, in their scale reconciled;
So it was with McMahon's flooded farm
After the storm, a ruin my eyes filed

Under marvels, as cattle broke the charm,
Blundering into ditches, rocking the double
Of hedge and cloud, until the painted calm

Restored itself. Now it's I who wake to trouble,
The future these converging rusty spears,
Like us, not meeting but inseparable.

The flock rises as one and disappears,
Swept off as I've seen them down Shannon winds
On pure wings that will never reach the years

Of inner lies, whose shadowy legion binds
Slaves in chain gangs once the bright playgrounds pall.
Paths no rocking horse rider ever finds

Lead to the heights of wonder, not the call
Of echoes; the fate of Orpheus may guide
Me in the Underground's hot-breathing hall

Or these un-Elysian fields, though my bride
Is not around to turn to, after all,
And here my children never come to ride.

– first appeared in *Outposts*

JACK NICHOLLS'

debut poetry pamphlet, *Meat Songs*,
is forthcoming from The Emma Press in 2017.
His work has appeared in such venues as the
Morning Star, Poems in Which, and *PANK,* among
others, and he has also won prizes for his short
plays. He runs the live lit cabaret Flim Nite,
and performs comedy with the sketch
group Beach Hunks.

THE DOLPHIN SINGS A LOVE SONG

(all language taken from the works of Dan Brown)

You stand wrapped in a towel and drip
on the neatly folded clothes
you'd set out the night before
I am a thirty-four-year-old
cult initiate, for you,
gazing down at the human skull
cradled in my palms like a stone
Although not overly handsome in a
classical sense, I am a silver-haired silver-tongued
political animal who has been anointed
with the slick look of a soap opera doctor, as a boy
I almost died treading water for hours,
on weekends I can be seen lounging
on the quad in blue jeans,   like a stone,
and my campus nickname, 'The Dolphin', is a
reference to both my affable nature
and my legendary ability to dive into a pool
and outmanoeuvre the entire opposing squad
in a water polo match. You stand wrapped
and   drip   drip
Clearly your father's good looks
have not skipped generations

Like a stone, I disappear

I am the son of a mathematics teacher
and a church organist, for years they have pursued me,
their persistence keeping me underground, labouring
beneath the earth like a
chthonic monster, almost died treading,

I still
have the body
of a swimmer
Like a stone, I disappear beneath
your foaming water, my spirit
gurgles heavenward,
depressed, you go to your closet
for a clean blouse and a skirt

RICHARD O'BRIEN's
second pamphlet, *The Emmores*,
was published by The Emma Press in
January 2014 and *A Bloody Mess* followed from
Valley Press in 2015. His work has featured
in *Oxford Poetry, Poetry London, The Salt Book of
Younger Poets* and *The Best British Poetry 2013*.
He is working on a Midlands3Cities-
funded PhD on Shakespeare and the
development of verse drama at the
University of Birmingham.

HAMMAM

Laid out like prime cuts on a heated slab,
three pasty British bodies, wracked with wealth,
jostled from mosque to simit-stall to cab,
each tacitly affronted by himself;
clutching our towels over shapeless abs,
we steam our shame off with our worldly pelf.
A man whose name I first mishear as 'Nigil'
is here to guide me through this solemn vigil.

His pot belly and towel are business dress.
I'm dunked and drenched in a warm and soothing rain.
First, I'm pulled down with a torturer's finesse;
head to my knees, then thrust to the wall again;
then, with a bristly glove and a firm caress,
he scrubs my body like a stubborn stain.
Each in his alcove, moulded and scraped by ritual,
purrs at the loosening grip of the habitual.

He strafes me with suds. He rubs me down like a dog.
His little finger deftly probes my ear.
He, motherly, rinses my hair. My pores unclog
a bead-curtain of sweat, and as it clears,
though I can't mute my inner monologue,
it joins the slow drip in the background. Here,
under the clean white dome which Sinan plotted,
I come to see how some can sleep unknotted.

After, we loll in robes, sip lemonade,
prepare to shoulder on the social shells
left in our lockers. And this too will fade,
as every system settles to its level:

our seats in the Caucasian cavalcade
remain reserved, as no one needs to tell
the man I paid to take away my dirt.
I tie my shoes. I button up my shirt.

ELIZABETH O'CONNELL-THOMPSON

is a Chicago-based Irish-American poet with all of her hyphens in place. She is the Literary Coordinator of the Chicago Publishers' Resource Center, where she leads the Wasted Pages Writers' Workshop series. Her work has been featured in *RHINO, Banshee,* and *The Wax Papers,* among others.

INVITATION ONLY

When they come knocking,
I take them by the hand that had been a fist moments before
and show them something beautiful –

> a black creek in the woods,
> a doe's skull in the field.

I lead them just far enough away that they can still see the house,
but not say if it is made of straw or stone.

While they are dipping their feet in the water
or watching how the sun sets on bone, I walk back
to bolt the door and light a fire,
holding myself as they had offered to do.

– first appeared in *Banshee*

GERALDINE O'KANE
is co-host of Purely Poetry,
a monthly poetry open-mic night run in
partnership with the Crescent Arts Centre. In
2015 she gave a TED Talk for TEDx Belfast
on poetry and mental health, and read at the
Poems Upstairs Series in association with Poetry
Ireland. Currently she is working towards her
first full collection of poetry and is a recipient of
the Artist Career Enhancement Scheme
(ACES) 2015/16 from the Arts Council
of Northern Ireland.

STARK...

You tell me over breakfast
your husband raped you.
I set down my cup
to look past your face
at shoulders protecting your heart.
'What do you want to do about it?'
'Nothing' you confirm twice.
I finish getting ready, leave for work.

In the car I run words, images back and forth
had I misheard anything, was there something amiss?
The white lines come close, disappear.
I pull over, breath, pound the steering wheel
embrace it, lay my head there for a second
breathe, pull out again.

Later I call you to see how you are
you assure me 'that's not what you said
it never happened, no, it never happened.'
I let it go but I've never forgotten.

MATTHEW PAUL

was born in New Malden, Surrey,
in 1966, and lives and works on the outskirts
of London. He was shortlisted for the Poetry
School/Pighog Press Pamphlet Competition
2013 and has had his poems published in a
variety of publications, including *Butcher's Dog*,
Magma, *Poetry Ireland Review*, *The Rialto* and *The
Best New British and Irish Poets 2016*. He co-edits
Presence haiku journal and has contributed
to *The Guardian*'s 'Country Diary'
column.

DUCKWALKING IN WEST BERLIN

Wangling a week's work with Teale's, who garden the British Sector quarters,
I'm assigned to learn the basics from Terry, who's been at it for years:
coining it in from the Federal Government's social generosity,
whilst earning a big enough wedge each summer to winter in Bali.

Last evening, Terry saw Miles Davis play his new album, *Tutu*,
and Chuck Berry, 'the best-ever support act', duckwalk 'like a nutter'.
Terry re-enacts the walk across the flowerbeds: head nodding forth
like a mid-river moorhen's; sunburnt kneecaps raking the bone-dry earth.

Later, I'm paired for weeding with Basildon Baz, at what he insists
was Eva Braun's house. After a lazy hour, we share a few spliffs
and dawdle round to sightsee the DDR wall guards, no older than
me, pacing up and down like the polar bears in the Tiergarten sun.

Baz and I degrade them further by mooning our Neo-Liberal arses;
as Rudolf Hess hangs himself in Spandau, inducing tanked-up Nazis
to bellow 'Horst Wessel' and slam along the towpath in Neukölln,
not sufficiently hammered yet to goose-step with total abandon.

JAMES PEAKE

was born in London and
educated at Bristol University and Trinity
College, Dublin. He has worked for several trade
publishers, including Penguin Random House
and Pan Macmillan, and has read for and edited
small magazines in the UK and the US. His
own poems have been published widely, most
recently in *The Next Review*.

THE MIDDLE PLACES

Silence can be fierce or expensive, a place
from which opposites confirm us
like the polished glass and the metal behind.

I love it when you relax with your legs across me.
It's easier to tune in to what you mean
when there's touch, when there's no between.

Something interior gurgles with health
and you prod yourself and laugh.
The TV watches us when it's off.

RACHEL PIERCEY

studied English Literature at St. Hugh's College, Oxford, where she won the Newdigate Prize in 2008. She has worked as a travel guide editor and Education Coordinator at The Poetry Society, and is now a freelance writer and editor. She has two pamphlets with The Emma Press, *The Flower and the Plough* (2013) and *Rivers Wanted* (2014). Rachel also writes and runs poetry workshops for children.

AN OVERBLOWN POEM ABOUT LOVE

Because it can see for two miles
I have set a peacock on the roof.

Its body is like a distilled sea
but more tempestuous and noisy.

Certain folk it regards as friends,
and then it hurries down to strut

around the dusty moat of yard
and make a revelation of its tail,

or simply does not pause in prising
insects from the slatted wood.

In many ways it is well-trained.
I mean, it is trained in many ways

by a variety of guests,
so it is tactically efficient.

Take this shape on the horizon:
slow, resolving, barrelling

into sight, towards the fence,
and how the peacock tenses, trembles,

starts to strike out with its claws,
and how it crashes through the yard

to scream at the stranger, gaining fast.

I'm contemplating something bad.

I have one hand upon the latch.
I have one hand upon the axe.

– first appeared in *The Poetry Review*

LAUREN POPE

is pursuing a Creative Writing
PhD at the University of Edinburgh,
where she organizes summer courses in Creative
Writing and British Literature. Her poetry has
appeared in various print and online publications
including *Etchings, Gutter, Magma,* and *The
Stockholm Review of Literature.* She is a recipient
of a Greenberg Poetry Fellowship, an
Orkney Writers' Bursary and the
Grierson Verse Prize.

MISCARRIAGE

I'm told
the moonstone
I carried
in the palm
of my hand
could not alone
will a living thing
to term,

and the eggs
consumed
upside down
on a Sunday
once held
the same possibility
for which I grieve.

Sometimes things
that do not exist
are real —
the way my ears
hear Etta James
sing 'Cadillac'
not 'At Last',
or how the opening
acoustics
to 'Little Wing'
are, to me, a mimesis
of drowning.

Announce this: today,
the colour of failure
is the robin's
sanguine throat.

– first appeared in *Gutter*

JODY PORTER

is the poetry editor of
Morning Star newspaper, and was
founding editor of poetry website *zafusy*
(2004-2008) which was chosen by the British
Library for online preservation. His work has
appeared in *Magma, South Bank Poetry,* and *The
International Times* as well as the anthologies *Best
British Poetry 2013* (Salt), *Catechism: Poems for Pussy
Riot,* and elsewhere. Originally from Essex,
he now lives in London and is involved in
the Stoke Newington Literary Festival.

LOOK

From the Café Auteur poems

The tiny ruins of a smashed glass catch your eye,
catch the evening as it rounds the Thames,
all orange-pink and sugar-muddled like a cocktail.

Time to knock off. Time to sweep away the pieces,
leave the bar to the nightshift's mercy, wave goodbye
to the crumpled tuxedo in its favourite chair.

The final credits are a denouement away.
You go to where people are as much themselves
as they can ever be and take their picture.

But not just them. A commuter is beatified
in rain. Flowers are drained to paper. It's spring,
but the flowers you show to the world are dying.

Even so the broken parts of the day
are brought back together by your hand.
The ruins of strangers even more so, look –

their petrol station bouquets, look! Defiant! Sad!
Look! You get home so very late when it rains
because you stop to look.

SAMUEL PRINCE

was born in Dewsbury
and lives and works in London.
His poems have appeared in various print
and online journals including *Cordite Poetry
Review, Lighthouse, Magma,* and *Orbis* as well as
the anthologies *Birdbook 2: Freshwater Habitats;
Coin Opera 2* and *Lives Beyond Us,*
all from Sidekick Books.

THE MAN FROM COOMA

The Australian feature showed him with burdizzo, a hog-tied calf
then in roly-poly pose with a Joey. He knows his Dickens,
knows his deuce; he's been a drongo, been a douche
and wears the professorial cardigan to prove it. He bids you
enter through a rattan fly curtain and offers you arak, a move
he learned from magi in withered cities. His string tie is winterised.
He's been a griller, grocery bagger, chuckwagon slopper,
and stowaway supremo but since waved sayonara to all that.
He calls his boutonniere his bandolier and dines in the milk bar
where he was a soda jerk, clutz and mopper extraordinaire.

His mother's chemise he caught sight of once in thundery weather.
He drives his Studebaker pickup to the southernmost promontory,
sits on the bonnet and holds forth on the first fleet Captains.
He chews on a Roi-Tan. He's more passion pit than passion play,
more penny dreadful than goldrush. He'd swap chandeliers
for tumbleweed, chauffeurs for rowel spurs and yes, he made tenure
but, by Jove, he remembers try-out failure for the forward line.
Fame never sustained him how he wanted, how you think it must.
It didn't have to be this way. He thought he had an agreement.
Everything we're sure about him is a McGuffin. The else matters more.

MATTHEW RICE

was born in Belfast in 1980.
He now lives in Carrickfergus, County
Antrim. He is currently studying for his BA
Honours in English Language and Literature.
Rice has published poems in magazines and
journals on both sides of the Atlantic. He was
one of six new poets showcased in a Poetry Day
Ireland reading organised by Poetry NI and
Poetry Ireland. He was long-listed
for the Seamus Heaney Award
for New Writing 2016.

AT THE LIGHTS

My friend says there are ways of seeing
that can reveal the world behind the world we see;
that, when accessed, will crumble away the cityscape
and show the reality behind the facade.
She's been reading a book called *The School of Seers*.
She's telling me this as we sit at the lights watching pedestrians

pass in front of the car from either side of the road,
dovetailing into space with expressive vacancy,
and I drift into thoughts of that opening battle sequence
in *Macbeth*, the strings that accompany it.
The sun's been in my eyes since we got in the car,
and everything has a sun stain as I close them tight

and allow the motes to melt into darkness.
I open my eyes again and we're moving;
my friend has gone silent. A single spot of rain
triggers the automatic wipers.

SAMANTHA RODEN

is a Lead Teacher and academic whose poetry
has featured in several online and print journals.
She performs her poetry at venues and festivals
in and around the Midlands and began her PhD
in Creative Writing in 2017. She is co-author
of *Philip Roth Through the Lens of Kepesh* (HEB,
2016) and she writes educational resources for
Cambridge University Press.

SHOVE YOUR TISSUES

The man wears chinos and a flannel shirt,
a zip-up fleece and odd socks:
one is more beige.

His face, as creased and faded as his shirt,
reminds me of *Guernica*, but without the light bulb,
or the nostrils.

If I did tell him about my penchant
for being led astray
by the man who holds a dog lead in one hand,
himself in the other,
he'd hurl himself at the space
where a window used to be,
then I'd have to counsel *him*.

He asks why I have my arms folded;
I ask why he doesn't.
'What would your present self say to your former self?'
'She'd say you're a prick.'
(*former self nods*.)

He writes down 'transference' and looks
at the clock I'm not supposed to notice
behind my head.

SARAH SIBLEY

was born in Bury St. Edmunds, Suffolk,
in 1985. She studied Creative Writing at
Lancaster and Wolverhampton Universities.
Her work has featured in *Agenda, Iota, Orbis,
Ink Sweat & Tears, And Other Poems,* and
Obsessed with Pipework. Her first pamphlet,
The Withering Room, is available
from Green Bottle Press.

LONE MAN STORIES

Up at High Winds farm by the slurry pit
we'd hide and seek in a thicket
ripped every night by storms –
the kind we don't get in these parts anymore.
For a time, stories of a lone man
wiped us out from the copse.
Rik Loader said he'd crossed back in,
showed us his souvenir – a knife,
its blade the width of my thigh.

At night I dreamt of the thicket;
in my hiding place a dead fox,
the lone man lost in a cloud of gnats.
Other times the startled pigs
and spooked horses tipped his mind
and he went staggering into the pit;
at the farm a single light kept vigil –
no stir from the brush,
a campfire burned to dust.

– first appeared in *The Withering Room,* (Green Bottle Press, 2015)

LUKE SMITH

grew up in Gloucestershire.
He received a Master's in Creative
Writing from the University of Oxford,
and he currently lives in Houston, Texas,
where he teaches English to 11 to
18-year-olds. He is co-editor
of *The Harlequin*.

ARTMAKING FOR YOUNG MEN

First, loosen. Become a swarm
of something you can breathe.
Take it in and hold communion.
Remember that your lungs are churches.

Host a funeral; make it a happy one
where people vomit on the oaken
pew-backs out of grief alone.
Learn to recognise heartbreak

in its fullest ululation and then
forget about it. Kick a clump of earth,
a stone, shin-bone a biscuit barrel.
Now you can tell them that you're sorry.

Understand small gestures
are among the very best we have
to offer, and offer them
a hand across the causeway.

Stay reckless; don't forget to breathe
as this is how the wake begins.
Be respectful and leave early.
Pocket something as you go.

JAYNE STANTON

is a teacher, tutor, and musician
from Leicestershire. Her poems have appeared
in various print and online magazines. She has
written commissions for a county museum and
for the University of Leicester's Centre for New
Writing, and she recently completed a poem
sequence about life in Leicester as part of a city
residency. Her pamphlet, *Beyond the Tune*, was
published by Soundswrite Press in 2014.

UNRESERVED COACH B

She's a talking timeline: post-war Norfolk to California Dream.
Her face is a contour map of the San Joaquin valley;
upstretched hands are Joshua trees to her storyboard

as Lancashire passes us by. She asks if I know the population
of Preston. I don't. We both endorse total hip replacement
for effective pain relief. Her smile is a Sacramento afternoon.
Her partner hides behind the compound eyes of Ray-Bans.

*

His name is Jack. Jack and his light sabre have dominion
over the carriage. They are on a galactic mission
through the restricted area around passengers' ankles,
all, that is, except those of his parents and sister.

Jack's sister doesn't have a name but she does have shoes
that flash like aircraft landing lights. She wants her fairy
to sit beside her. Mummy says her fairy is tired.
Her fairy is sleeping in the overhead luggage rack
and won't come down 'til Crewe.

*

A swarm of yellow and black, they infest the carriage,
colonising empty seats. The air is thick
with their pheromones. There's a buzz
around four-packs of Carling, bottles of Jack Daniels.

On a loop, Elvis Costello announces,
        Oliver's army are on their way-ay.

I attempt to Google Wolves + fixtures
but Wi-Fi is lost property between stations.

*

At Birmingham New Street my suitcase drags its wheels
and escalators have stopped reaching for the light.

JAMES TREVELYAN

grew up in the Midlands
and now lives in London.
His debut pamphlet, *DISSOLVE
to: L.A.,* was published by
The Emma Press in 2016.

COUGAR

Cougar, the number one pilot in flight school, goes into shock
as an enemy plane trains a missile on him. Pete 'Maverick'
Mitchell guides him back to base and Cougar 'turns in his
wings' (*Top Gun,* 1986).

Guide me in, Maverick,
you live your life in the skies and between your legs,
and I've seen you rouse a bar full of pilots and blondes
into singing your song. You're a one-off, Maverick,
like your father was, and if I manage to stay
on your wing I know you'll take me all the way in.

Guide me in, Iceman,
slide me on a frozen jet stream,
throw this catamount down the mountain,
let me tumble in your avalanche and come to
rest on the steep rock of your face,
sleep curled in its cave for a cool decade.

Guide me in, Jester,
call me floozie, milf, molester;
call me cradle-snatcher, spring-semester.
Jester, *meow* at my comebacks,
call me pussycat in front of the guys. Call my name,
Jester, look me in the eyes, and I'll call yours.

Guide me in, Goose,
fly me in formation, pull the ejectors,
be my mate. You were truly hatched
of a golden egg. Teach us the ways
of monogamy and treat me to a rest
in the downy feather of your pit.

Guide me in, Hollywood,
with your turbo complexion
and hair metal. I'll follow the shine
of your teeth and behind,
Hollywood, your rudderless bronze
chassis is catnip to me.
Guide me in, Wolfman,
and I'll cling to your roar – ride
on your back like an oxpecker – because
I've seen your clod paws thwack
a volleyball hard enough to know
I lack every inch of you.

Guide me in, Sundown,
you always had my number and know
I'm no growler, no alleycat. That last evening
you reached inside my squinting eyes, bounced
around the cockpit, and brought me down,
belly up, engines purring.

– first appeared in *DISSOLVE to:* L.A. (The Emma Press, 2016)

DEBORAH TURNBULL's
work has been published in *Ink Sweat
& Tears*, and in the second volume of *The
Embodiment Journal*. She has been collaborating
with The Fortune Cats, and her poetry and
scripts appear in various digital art installations,
including in Somerset House for the Art of Bots
festival. Deborah is also a hair and
makeup artist, and lives with her
family in Brighton.

FOUNDLING

The expanse of an innocent
face is a screen to see
clouds panning, pylons, billboards.
(You'll be on every one of those, sweetheart.)

Those huge eyes, as though deadly
nightshade was dabbed
in their imploring corners.
You won't need any of that

where you're going, belladonna.
Your sweet excess, deep Cupid's
bow, has dollar signs all over it.
A stray lock blows across your face,

concealing you for a second, alluring
little thing. I'll be your agency.
Put your name in lights, and in
the mouths of strangers, baby.

CAROLYN WAUDBY

is an award-winning journalist and lecturer
with a particular interest in travel writing. She
specialises in artistic collaborations and her
poetry has appeared on film and in exhibitions,
in addition to publication in magazines such
as *Magma, The Reader,* and *Mslexia*. She is
currently working on poems inspired by Frida
Kahlo.

DALI'S ROSE

This rose is open, the sun cannot steal its dew,
no stem tethers it to the ground. It is a cloud
on which we ride over Andalucian hills
and parched terracotta villages on the landscape's
lumber curve. Duchovny, when asked to cite the most
pleasing part of a woman, chose the depression
of the sacrum, just above the buttock's fissure.
He could build a house on it, he said. You agreed.
Two figures stand like nine-pins, apart, heads inclined,
their shadows thin. The rose with its red perfection
is cover from the sun's inexhaustible stare.
No sickness, invisible worm, or howling storm.

– first appeared in *Matter*

KATE WISE

has been published
in various magazines in print and online,
including *Poems in Which, Ink Sweat & Tears,
And Other Poems, Structo* and *Haverthorn*. Her
poem 'Urinal Blocks' was a winner in the
Members' Poems competition in the summer
issue of *Poetry News* in 2016. Her work has
appeared in three anthologies published
by The Emma Press.

DEATH COMES ASKING

You need to stop thinking.

What was it? Those are pearls that were –
Those are pearls that –
Those are...

They are not.
But stones, perhaps?
And when we plant a human, how long...?

Where is the circle in which you believed?
Won't gold hinges break it?
How long does varnish take to...

If I come to you and speak, do you hear me?
Will another stone help?
Why

     – and for a moment all is quiet –

Then Death comes, asking.

       So – and here he reaches out a soft arm
       and what might be sympathy –
       how did he go?
       Did you do all you could?
       Did you sing and feed him poetry?
       Were his lips kept wet?
       Did you shoo the Raven from his window?
       And he could just be in the next room –
       don't you think?
       And you'll always have the memories.
       As long as you don't let them fade, that is.

Did he grow devil-warding Elder?
You say there was a Green Man?
But perhaps he was careless of fairy circles?
Refused to throw salt over?

Well then, it sounds, he says, shrugging
that you almost certainly did all you could. Probably.
Don't you agree?

Probably. Almost.

And you have these words.
Take them.
Store them. Write them down. Shore them up
against...
Let them circulate. Again and again and again and.
You mustn't feel guilty.
You didn't?
I'm sorry. But still,
don't.

In the batpurpled evening
and the splintered night
and the still small quiet of the morning's weak light
— in your going out,
and your coming in.
They will be here, for you.
Waiting. Haunting. Don't be afraid...
be afraid...
be afraid...

Afraid.

You must stop thinking! Please stop thinking.
Stop thinking.

Stop.

LUKE KENNARD,

Senior Lecturer in Creative Writing
at the University of Birmingham, won the Eric
Gregory Award in 2005 for his first collection, *The
Solex Brothers*. His second collection, *The Harbour
Beyond The Movie*, was shortlisted for the 2007 Forward
Prize for Best Collection, making him the youngest
ever poet to be nominated. In 2014 he was named as
one of the Poetry Book Society's Next Generation
Poets. His latest collection, *Cain*, was released to
critical acclaim in 2016, and his debut novel, *The
Transition* is new from Fourth Estate.

TODD SWIFT

is the Montreal-born, British
founder-director of Eyewear Publishing,
based in London and now in its 6th year. His own
poems are Selected by Salmon in Ireland and Marick
in the USA. He has edited or co-edited over a dozen
anthologies since 1988, including *The Poet's Quest
For God*. His latest pamphlet is *Madness & Love In Maida
Vale* (2016). His PhD is from the UEA, on style in mid-
century British poets, notably Tiller and Prince. His
essays on poetry have recently appeared in academic
publications from Palgrave and the University of
Liverpool, as well as in *Poetry* magazine and *Poetry
London*. He was included in *The Oxford Companion
to Modern Poetry in English*. He is the 2017/18
Writer-in-residence for Pembroke College,
Cambridge University.

☐☐ EYEWEAR PUBLISHING